The story of Christmas

A book of 30 Bible readings and notes to
help you worship and pray

This book was written by **Suzy Edmundson** and **Derek
Thompson**, with a little help and encouragement from
friends. It was edited by **Tony Phelps-Jones**.

Published by Scripture Union, 207–209 Queensway, Bletchley, MK2 2EB, England.

Email: info@scriptureunion.org.uk
Internet: www.scriptureunion.org.uk

First published in this revision by Scripture Union in 2004.
ISBN 1 85999 063 7

Causeway PROSPECTS is a division of PROSPECTS for People with Learning Disabilities, and their address is PO Box 351, Reading, RG30 4XQ. Phone 0118 9516 978. Email: causeway@prospects.org.uk

About Causeway PROSPECTS: Causeway PROSPECTS provides resource materials and training to equip churches for effective outreach and ministry among people with learning disabilities. It also runs holiday weekends and special ministry at Spring Harvest and the Keswick Convention.

British Library Cataloguing-in-Publication Data: a catalogue record for this book is available from the British Library.

Scripture portions are taken from The Holy Bible: English Version for the Deaf (published as the Easy-to-Read Version) © 1995 by World Bible Translation Center, Inc. and used with permission. Internet: www.wbtc.com

Icons © Widgit Software Ltd 2002, developed by the Rebus Symbol Development Project, designed by Cate Detheridge, and used with kind permission.

Cover design by David Lund Design, Milton Keynes.

Printed and bound in Great Britain by goodmanbaylis, The Trinity Press, Worcester, UK.

✤ **Scripture Union**: We are an international Christian charity working with churches in more than 130 countries providing resources to bring the good news about Jesus Christ to children, young people and families – and to encourage them to develop spiritually through the Bible and prayer. As well as our network of volunteers, staff and associates who run holidays, church-based events and school Christian groups, we produce a wide range of publications and support those who use our resources through training programmes.

How to use this book

 These daily notes are intended to help you to worship and to pray.   Each day there is a short reading from the Bible, some thoughts and a prayer.

 The readings are from the *Easy-to-Read Version* (ETRV), a very clear and simple translation of the Bible.   The reading printed each day is quite short.   A longer reading is also given if you would like to read more using your own Bible.

The Bible, which is sometimes called the Word of God, is not really one book but a whole library of many books.   The 66 books were written by many people that God spoke to at different times.   At the front of the Bible you will find a list of the titles of all the books in the Bible and the page number where each book begins.

To help you find your way around such a big book, little groups of one or two sentences have been numbered, and then groups of those sentences have been collected into chapters.

So how do you find the one or two sentences that you want in the Bible?   Let's say you want to find Matthew 5:5,6.   That means you need to look in the book called Matthew, in chapter number 5 and verses 5 and 6.

You can find Matthew in the lists of books at the front of the Bible.   In the *Easy-to-Read Bible*, Matthew starts on page 1109.   So when you have turned to the beginning of Matthew you then search for chapter 5, which is on page 1113.   Look down the page until you see the numbers 5 and 6.   Those are the sentences (or verses) that you need.

When you do your Bible reading, try to spend a few extra minutes praying and worshipping. Prayer is talking and listening to God. You can do this aloud or without using words. You can pray on your own or with friends. Worship is telling God how much you love him, through words or songs, or things you do. This can be singing in church, but it's a lot more than that, too. It's about enjoying the wonderful world God has made. It's about how we speak to each other. It's about how we live our lives.

As you pray you can:

 thank God for his goodness and his help;

 tell God how great he is, and that you love him;

 ask God to help you, your friends, your family and other people.

If you are a helper using this book with someone who does not read, you will find guidance notes at the end.

The *Easy-to-Read Version* of the Bible is available to buy from Causeway PROSPECTS.

The story of Christmas

1 The first Christmas

Mary ... gave birth to her first son (Jesus). There was not enough room for them in the house. So Mary wrapped the baby with pieces of cloth and laid the baby in a box where cattle are fed. Luke 2:7 (Full reading Luke 2:4–7)

It was the first Christmas – the day the baby Jesus was born. Mary must have thought her baby was the most wonderful baby ever. And she was right. The baby Jesus was God's own Son.

But this wasn't how the story began. The story began before the world was even made. In this book we'll find out what the Bible tells us about the whole story right from the beginning.

Father God, thank you for your Son Jesus. Please help me to understand what the Bible tells me about Jesus. Amen.

2 The beginning

 Before the world began, the Word [Jesus] was there. The Word [Jesus] was there with God. John 1:1 (Full reading John 1:1–3)

 God and his Son Jesus were together in heaven. They were there in heaven before there was a world, before there were any people.

Then God and his Son Jesus decided to make the world. They decided to make a world with people in it, people like us. God and Jesus wanted people like us to be in their family.

God and Jesus stayed together in heaven until Jesus came from heaven to our world. Jesus was born as a baby and grew up with ordinary people like us.

 Lord Jesus, thank you for making the world, and for making me part of it. Thank you that people are so important to you. Amen.

3 Jesus made everything

All things were made through him [Jesus].
Nothing was made without him.
John 1:3 (Full reading John 1:1–3)

Who do you think made the world we live in?
Jesus did!

Jesus helped God make the ground we walk on.
Together they made the sky and the sun and the
moon, the trees and the flowers and the wind
and the rain. Jesus and God made everything
we can see around us. They made people. And
everything they made was good.

Think about something you really like. Your
favourite flower or a beautiful animal. Or
someone who really helps you. You can thank
Jesus for everything he made.

Lord Jesus, thank you for all the wonderful
things you made for us. Thank you for
everything. Amen.

The Lord hoped for justice, but there was only killing. The Lord hoped for fairness, but there were only cries from people being treated badly.
Isaiah 5:7 (Full reading Isaiah 5:5–7)

Jesus and his Father God made the world and all the people. Everything was good. But people spoiled it all. They started to fight and be mean to one another. They took no notice of God and they did bad things. This made God sad.

God wanted people to know how sad he was because of what they were doing. So he chose a man called Isaiah to talk to the people. Isaiah warned the people about the bad things they were doing. Isaiah told them how God was going to put things right.

Father God, help me to be sorry when I do bad things. Help me to do only good things. Amen.

5 God's wonderful love

 God loved the world so much that he gave his only Son. God gave his Son so that every person that believes in him would not be lost, but have life forever.
John 3:16 (Full reading John 3:16,17)

 God saw all the bad things people were doing. God was angry.

But God still loves people, even if they do bad things. He wanted people to stop doing bad things. So God sent his own Son Jesus to show people how to do only good things. Jesus died on a cross. He was punished so that people can be forgiven for the bad things they do. Because of this, everyone can be part of God's family forever.

 Father God, thank you for loving people so much. Thank you for sending your Son Jesus. Thank you that I can be forgiven because Jesus died on the cross. Amen.

God will give a son to us. This son will be responsible for leading the people. His name will be 'Wonderful Counsellor, Powerful God, Father Who Lives Forever, Prince of Peace' ... this king will use goodness and fair judgment to rule the kingdom forever and ever.
Isaiah 9:6,7 (Full reading Isaiah 9:2–7)

Isaiah lived a long time before Jesus was born. But God told Isaiah things about Jesus. God told Isaiah that Jesus would be wonderful – too wonderful for words. Think how wonderful God is. That's how wonderful Jesus is too!

Isaiah said Jesus would be a wonderful counsellor. A good counsellor is like a very special friend who listens when you are in trouble and then helps you. Jesus always listens when we pray. Jesus helps us when we are in trouble.

Lord Jesus, you are wonderful. Thank you for being my special friend and helper. Thank you, Jesus, for being my wonderful counsellor. Amen.

God will give a son to us. This son will be responsible for leading the people. His name will be 'Wonderful Counsellor, Powerful God, Father Who Lives Forever, Prince of Peace' ... this king will use goodness and fair judgment to rule the kingdom for ever and ever.
Isaiah 9:6,7 (Full reading Isaiah 9:2–7)

Jesus is our wonderful counsellor. He listens to us, and then he helps us.

But there's something else. God is angry when we do bad things. We are in trouble with God!

When this happens, Jesus will ask his Father God not to be angry with us. He will ask God to forgive us. But we have to say sorry to God.

Because of Jesus we can tell God when we have done something wrong. God will forgive us.

Father God, thank you for Jesus. Thank you that even when I do bad things Jesus always speaks up for me. Amen.

God will give a son to us. This son will be responsible for leading the people. His name will be 'Wonderful Counsellor, Powerful God, Father Who Lives Forever, Prince of Peace' ... This king will use goodness and fair judgment to rule the kingdom for ever and ever.
Isaiah 9:6,7 (Full reading Isaiah 9:2–7)

Jesus asks God to forgive us when we do bad things. Then we can be close friends with God again. God will not be angry or cross with us anymore. It's like when we have a quarrel with a special friend, or with one of our family. It spoils everything. But if we forgive each other we can be friends again. Everything will be peaceful and good again like it was before.

Jesus is called the Prince of Peace. The special peace that Jesus gives us is knowing we are friends with God.

Lord Jesus, thank you for the peace you give to me. Thank you for making me a friend of God. Amen.

9 Trusting Jesus

God will give a son to us. This son will be responsible for leading the people. His name will be 'Wonderful Counsellor, Powerful God, Father who lives Forever, Prince of Peace' ... This king will use goodness and fair judgment to rule the kingdom for ever and ever.
Isaiah 9:6,7 (Full reading Isaiah 9:2–7)

Every country has somebody in charge. It might be a king or queen. It might be a prime minister or a president. They usually try to do the right things. But often they make mistakes. They do things that are bad or unfair.

Jesus isn't like that. Jesus is a very different kind of king. Jesus is always good. Jesus loves us and is always fair to us.

We can trust Jesus. Jesus will never leave us or forget us.

Lord Jesus, thank you that you are such a good king. You are always fair and loving. Please be in charge of my life. Amen.

10 The angel Gabriel

God sent the angel Gabriel to a virgin [unmarried] girl that lived in Nazareth, a town in Galilee ... Her name was Mary.
Luke 1:26,27 (Full reading Luke 1:26–28)

God chose a woman called Mary to be Jesus' mother. What a very special job to do!

So God sent an angel called Gabriel to tell Mary what was going to happen. Can you imagine what it would be like to see an angel?

Angels bring messages from God at very special times. Gabriel was a very special angel. In heaven, it was part of Gabriel's job to stay close to God and praise him. Gabriel came to earth to speak to Mary.

Father God, it must be wonderful to be close to you in heaven and praise you like Gabriel does. Thank you that you use ordinary people like Mary and like me, as well as angels, to do the things you want. Amen.

11 A job to do

The angel said to her, 'Don't be afraid, Mary, because God is very pleased with you. Listen! You will become pregnant. You will give birth to a baby boy. And you will name him Jesus'.
Luke 1:30,31 (Full reading Luke 1:30–33)

Mary was an ordinary young woman who loved God. When she saw the angel, she didn't know what was going to happen. The angel did not want to frighten Mary. So the angel told her not to be afraid, and then the angel told her the amazing news.

Mary would be a good mother for God's Son Jesus. Jesus would need a mother who would love him and look after him while he was growing up.

God had a special job for Mary to do. God has something for each one of us to do.

Father God, thank you for choosing Mary to look after your Son Jesus. Please show me what special job you have for me to do. Amen.

12 Doing what God wants

Mary said, 'I am the servant girl of the Lord (God). Let this thing you have said happen to me!' Then the angel went away.
Luke 1:38 (Full reading Luke 1:34–38)

Mary was engaged to be married to a man called Joseph. The two of them probably spent lots of time together making plans for the time when they would be married. Now it was all going to be different because there was a baby on the way.

Mary believed the angel and trusted God. So all Mary said was, 'Let this thing you have said happen to me'. Mary obeyed God. She was happy to do what God wanted her to do.

God wouldn't let her down. God was going to help Mary while she was pregnant with her special baby.

Father God, I am happy to do what you want me to do. But sometimes I am afraid when things happen to me. Help me to trust you and know that you love me. Amen.

18

13 Doing the right thing

... an angel of the Lord came to Joseph in a dream. The angel said, 'Joseph, son of David, don't be afraid to accept Mary to be your wife'. Matthew 1:20 (Full reading Matthew 1:18–25)

God had sent his angel Gabriel to Mary to tell her she was going to have a baby. Now he sent the angel to Joseph.

Mary and Joseph were engaged to be married. Then Joseph found out that Mary was pregnant. Joseph loved Mary. But now he didn't know what to do.

The angel told Joseph that it was right to marry Mary. Mary hadn't done anything wrong. The baby was God's Son.

It is sometimes hard to know what is the right thing to do. If you don't know what to do, ask God to help you. He will make things clearer for you.

Father God, thank you that Joseph did the right thing. Help me to know what are the right things to do every day. Amen.

14 Special babies

The angel said to Mary, ' ... your relative Elizabeth is pregnant. She is very old, but she is going to have a son. Everyone thought she could not have a baby, but she has been pregnant now for six months!'
Luke 1:35,36 (Full reading Luke 1:5–25,35–37)

Do you remember how Gabriel, the angel from God, came to Mary? Gabriel told her that she was going to have a baby called Jesus.

Gabriel also told Mary that her cousin Elizabeth was going to have a baby as well. Elizabeth's baby was going to be special too. He was going to be called John. When he grew up it would be his job to tell people to get ready to meet Jesus.

Mary and Elizabeth were both going to have very special babies.

Father God, thank you for Elizabeth and Mary and their special babies. Please watch over anyone who is getting ready to have a baby. Please keep them and their babies safe. Amen.

15 Mary visits Elizabeth

Mary got up and went quickly to a town in the hill country of Judea. She went into Zechariah's house and greeted Elizabeth. When Elizabeth heard Mary's greeting, the unborn baby inside Elizabeth jumped ... Elizabeth said with a loud voice, 'God has blessed you (Mary) more than any other woman. And God has blessed the baby which you will give birth to.'
Luke 1:39–42 (Full reading Luke 1:39–45)

Elizabeth did not know about Mary and Jesus. She did not know that Jesus was God's Son. But when she saw Mary, Elizabeth's baby jumped inside her. God told Elizabeth that Mary's baby was his Son Jesus.

Elizabeth was so excited and happy that she shouted out loud. Elizabeth talked about how special Mary and Jesus were. Elizabeth was thrilled that Mary had come to stay with her!

Father God, it is exciting to hear about the great things you have done. Help me to share my excitement about Jesus with other people. Amen.

16 Someone to help

Mary stayed with Elizabeth for about three months. Then Mary went home.
Luke 1:56 (Full reading Luke 1:46–56)

Mary went to see her cousin Elizabeth and stayed with her for three months.

Mary was young so perhaps Elizabeth helped her a lot. Mothers often get tired when their babies are growing inside them. God didn't want Mary or Elizabeth to be on their own. God brought them together to help each other.

Do you know someone who is lonely or not well? Perhaps you could visit them. Or you could send a card. You could cheer them up. You could pray.

Father God, thank you for making sure we have people to help us, especially if we are having a difficult or hard time or if we are worried or sick. Please help anyone who is not feeling well today, and people who are on their own. Amen.

17 God knows everything

So Joseph left Nazareth, a town in Galilee. He went to the town of Bethlehem in Judea ... While Joseph and Mary were in Bethlehem, the time came for Mary to have the baby.
Luke 2:4–6 (Full reading Luke 2:1–7)

After Mary left Elizabeth's house she went back home. She married Joseph, the man she was engaged to. Soon it would be time for Mary to have her baby.

Then the people in charge of the country made everyone go back to the place where they were born. Everyone had to write their names in a book so that they could be counted. So Mary and Joseph went to Bethlehem.

God always knew that Jesus was going be born in Bethlehem and he had already told people about it. If you like, you can read about it, in Micah 5:2.

Father God, when I am worried or afraid, help me to remember that you always know what is going to happen. Amen.

18 Jesus is born

While Joseph and Mary were in Bethlehem, the time came for Mary to have the baby. She gave birth to her first son (Jesus). There was not enough room for them in the house. So Mary wrapped the baby with pieces of cloth and laid the baby in a box where cattle are fed.

Luke 2:6,7 (Full reading Luke 2:1–7)

This is how Jesus came into our world. Until then he had been with Father God in heaven.

Jesus was a very special baby. Everyone who came to see Jesus knew how special he was, even when he was a baby. Seeing Jesus made a difference to their lives. Jesus still makes a difference to people's lives today.

Father God, thank you that Jesus came down from heaven to be born as a baby. Thank you that Jesus makes my life different. Help me to tell other people about it. Amen.

19 Angels praise God

An angel of the Lord (God) stood before the shepherds ... The angel said to them, '... Today your Saviour was born in David's town. He is Christ, the Lord.' ... Then a very large group of angels from heaven joined the first angel ... praising God, saying: 'Praise God in heaven, and on earth let there be peace to the people that please God'.
Luke 2:9–14 (Full reading Luke 2:8–15)

We get excited when a new baby is born. We want everyone to hear about it! God wanted everybody to know about Jesus.

When the shepherds saw the angels they were afraid. Who wouldn't be? But when the angels told them Jesus had been born, the shepherds were really excited. They wanted to go and see him! Then a great crowd of angels started praising God – singing about how great God is.

For your prayer today, why don't you praise God like the angels did, just by telling him how great and wonderful he is?

20 Joyful shepherds

So the shepherds went quickly and found Mary and Joseph. The baby was lying in the feeding box ... The shepherds went back to their sheep, praising God and thanking him for everything that they had seen and heard.
Luke 2:16,20 (Full reading Luke 2:15–20)

Do you remember telling God in your prayers how wonderful he is and how happy you feel about Jesus? This is just how the shepherds felt, too. All the way back home, they kept on talking about how great and good God is and thanking him for the wonderful thing they had seen.

God wants us to be people who praise him every day. Telling God how good he is makes him happy and it's good for us too!

Father God, I praise you because you are such a great and loving God. Please send your Holy Spirit to fill me with your joy so I keep praising you every day. Amen.

21 Thank God for babies

Joseph and Mary brought Jesus to Jerusalem so they could present him to the Lord (God).
Luke 2:22 (Full reading Luke 2:22–24)

Nowadays some people take their new babies to church to be baptised or dedicated to God. All babies are special, and we want them to be part of God's family. We want to thank God for babies.

Back in those days, when families had their first baby they used to take the baby to the temple (church) to be shown to God. This is how they said thank you to God for their baby. They used to thank God with a small offering (like a present) of two pigeons. So that was what Mary and Joseph did.

Babies and children are an important part of our churches.

Father God, thank you that all babies are so special to you. I pray for the babies and children in church as they grow up in your family. Amen.

22 God kept his promise

 **A man named Simeon lived in Jerusalem. He
was a good man that truly worshipped God.
Simeon was waiting for the time when God
would come to help Israel (the Jews) ... The Holy
Spirit ... led Simeon to the temple.**
Luke 2:25–27 (Full reading Luke 2:25–35)

 Simeon was a very old man. All his life he had
been waiting for God to send Jesus. God made
it happen. When Mary and Joseph brought
Jesus to the temple, Simeon was there. Think
how wonderful it must have been for Simeon,
holding God's Son in his arms!

God cared about the old man Simeon and made
him very happy. Simeon told Mary and Joseph
about Jesus being special.

 **Saying or singing this song is a good way to
praise God:**

> **Thank you Father for your love for me.**
> **Thank you for Jesus.**
> **You are faithful and you never change.**
> **How I love you, Father, how I love you.**

23 Anna talks about Jesus

**Anna, a prophetess, was there at the temple ...
Anna was very old. She had been married for
seven years. Then her husband died and she
lived alone. She was now 84 years old. Anna
was always at the Temple ... She worshipped
God by fasting and praying day and night ... She
... talked about Jesus to all the people who were
waiting for God to free Jerusalem.**
Luke 2:36–38 (Full reading Luke 2:36–38)

A prophet is someone who knows what God
wants to say, then tells the people those things.
Anna was a woman prophet – a prophetess.
When Anna prayed to God, God would tell her the
things he was going to do. So when Anna saw the
baby Jesus she knew straightaway who he was!

Then Anna told other people. People believed
what she said. God often tells us things through
what other people say to us.

**Father God, thank you for Anna and for the
people who tell us about you. Help them to
speak clearly and help me to understand what
they say. Amen.**

24 Finding Jesus

After Jesus was born, some wise men from the east came to Jerusalem. The wise men asked people, 'Where is the new baby that is the king of the Jews? We saw the star that shows he was born. We saw the star rise in the sky in the east. We came to worship him.'
Matthew 2:1,2 (Full reading Matthew 2:1,2)

The wise men lived a long way away from Bethlehem where the baby Jesus was born. The wise men knew all about stars. So God sent them a special star to show them where Jesus was.

There are lots of stars in the sky, aren't there? But God's star was different from all the rest. The wise men knew it was special. When it began to move they followed it.

It is important for every person to find Jesus. They do not need to travel far like the wise men. They only need to pray for Jesus to be their friend.

Father God, please help people to search for you and find you. Amen.

25 Wise men worship Jesus

The wise men came to the house where the baby was. They saw the baby with his mother Mary. The wise men bowed down and worshipped the baby. The wise men opened the gifts they brought for the baby. They gave the baby treasures of gold, frankincense and myrrh.
Matthew 2:11 (Full reading Matthew 2:9–11)

When a new baby is born, friends and family often bring presents. The wise men brought presents for Jesus.

But this was different. The wise men knew that Jesus was special. They came to worship him.

The presents the wise men brought were the very best things they had to give. Just think about these wise, important men kneeling down to worship a tiny child. Seeing Jesus was the most wonderful thing that had ever happened to them. They were filled with joy.

Father God, thank you that the wise men were so excited about Jesus. Thank you that I can be excited about Jesus, and worship him. Amen.

... The wise men opened the gifts they brought for the baby. They gave the baby treasures of gold, frankincense and myrrh.
Matthew 2:11 (Full reading Matthew 2:9–11)

The wise men brought treasures. Treasures aren't just ordinary presents. Treasures are the best things you have, the most special things. The wise men brought gold. Gold is very precious and expensive. Gold was a gift for a king. Bringing gold showed that the wise men knew Jesus was a king.

We can't all bring gold to Jesus. But we can do our best to please him.

What can you do today to help other people? Doing things like that shows how much we love Jesus. To Jesus, that matters just as much as gold.

Father God, thank you that the wise men brought the most precious thing they could find for your Son Jesus. Help me use the things I do well to please you like they did. Amen.

27 Frankincense

 ... The wise men opened the gifts they brought for the baby. They gave the baby treasures of gold, frankincense and myrrh.
Matthew 2:11 (Full reading Matthew 2:9–11)

 The wise men gave Jesus frankincense. Frankincense is a very special perfume. When it is burned, it makes a wonderful smell.

People in some churches burn frankincense or other perfumes. It helps them to worship God.

We can all worship God. We can all tell God that we love him. You can do that now as you pray.

 Father God, thank you for listening to our prayers. Help us to think before we pray, and to tell you how special you are. How I love you, Father. Amen.

28 Myrrh

... The wise men opened the gifts they brought for the baby. They gave the baby treasures of gold, frankincense and myrrh.
Matthew 2:11 (Full reading Matthew 2:9–11)

The wise men gave Jesus myrrh. Myrrh is another kind of perfume. People used myrrh to make oil. Oil made with myrrh was only ever given to very special people – people who were going to do wonderful things for God.

The myrrh the wise men brought was a special oil for Jesus. Jesus was going to do the most wonderful thing ever. Jesus was going to show people like us how to belong to God's family forever.

Do you know someone who is very special, or someone who has done wonderful things for God? In your prayers today thank God for that person. Pray for God to help them.

Father God, thank you for the special people in my life. Please send your Holy Spirit to help them every day. Amen.

29 God kept Jesus safe

After the wise men left, an angel of the Lord came to Joseph in a dream. The angel said, 'Get up! Take the baby and his mother and escape to Egypt ... Herod wants to kill him'.
Matthew 2:13 (Full reading Matthew 2:13–16)

Do you remember how the wise men brought gold for Jesus because Jesus was going to be a king?

But there was a king in the country already, a man called Herod. Herod was a wicked man who did a lot of very bad things. Herod certainly did not want Jesus to be king instead of him. So Herod wanted to kill the baby Jesus. But God sent an angel to warn Joseph. Joseph took Mary and Jesus to another country where they would be safe.

God loves you as much as he loves Jesus. He will care for you and keep you safe.

Father God, thank you for your special care for Jesus and his family. Thank you for keeping me safe. Amen.

After Herod died, an angel of the Lord came to Joseph in a dream. This happened while Joseph was in Egypt. The angel said, 'Get up! Take the baby and his mother and go to Israel. The people that were trying to kill the baby are now dead'.

Matthew 2:19,20 (Full reading Matthew 2:19–23)

Joseph, Mary and Jesus stayed in Egypt for two years. Then the bad king Herod died. The angel told Joseph that he could take his family home.

Jesus grew up in a town called Nazareth with his family. He had brothers and sisters. Their father Joseph was a carpenter, making things out of wood. Jesus helped Joseph to make things like tables and chairs. People liked Jesus, and Jesus pleased God.

Father God, it's lovely to think of Jesus growing up in a family. It means Jesus knows what it's like for us to be in families. Please help everyone in my family to be loving and helpful. Amen.

Key Words

Amen We usually say this at the end of prayers and it means 'That's my prayer too'.

Cross To be cross is to be angry, bad-tempered.

Cross A cross is two big pieces of wood in the shape of a cross. Jesus was nailed to a cross when he was killed.

Fair Being fair is doing the right thing, treating all people well.

Faith Believing that God will keep his promises.

Faithful Doing what you say you will do.
Believing that God will keep his promises.

Forgive When you forgive someone who has hurt you, you're not cross with them anymore.

Glorious Something wonderful that shows how great or powerful God is.

Honest Doing everything right, telling the truth.

Jealous A jealous person wants something that belongs to someone else, or wants to keep things to themselves, without sharing.

Peace /
peaceful   Quiet, calm, not worrying.

Prayer   What you say to God or Jesus when you
                      pray.

Promise   Something you say you will do for
                      somebody.

Punish   To make someone suffer or pay for doing
                      something wrong.

Punishment What happens to a person who is caught
                      doing something bad or wrong.

Selfish   Thinking only about yourself.

Sin / Sins   Bad things people do that make God sad
                      and hurt other people.

Trust   Believing that someone will do what they
                      say.

Worship   Telling God how much you love him
                      through words or songs or things you do.

Notes for carers and helpers

These Bible notes are designed to help a wide a range of people who need extra help. It's impossible to tailor Bible notes to fit everyone's needs. But our hope is that many who have some level of visual or intellectual disability or just need a simpler approach can be helped to pray and read the Bible regularly through this series.

Some people will be able to use these notes without any help from others. But if you are the carer or helper of someone needing some assistance with using them, here are a few pointers which may be useful to you.

Before you begin, ask the Holy Spirit to help communicate the main thought from each reading and note to the person you are reading with. God through the Holy Spirit can communicate on levels that we cannot! Part of the Holy Spirit's role is to make Jesus real to people and you are working in partnership with him.

Make sure you have the person's full attention before starting to read. Think about how you can eliminate auditory or visual distractions in the environment such as TV or other people. Try to find a quiet place. Use eye contact to maintain good connection.

Read slowly and clearly, pausing where suitable. Facial expressions, hand and body movements can all help to underline the meaning of the material. Encourage whatever response is appropriate, particularly in prayer and praise.

Use your knowledge of the person to assess how much is being understood, how much clarification might be needed and how to best make applications more relevant.

Make your time together an opportunity for learning and fellowship for both of you.

Other titles in the Bible Prospects series:

Being like Jesus

Songs of praise

God gives new life

Scripture Union produces a wide range of Bible reading notes for people of all ages and Bible-based material for small groups. SU publications are available from any Christian bookshop. For information and to request free samples and a free catalogue of Bible resources:

- phone SU's mail order line: local rate number 08450 706 006

- email info@scriptureunion.org.uk

- fax 01908 856020

- log on to www.scriptureunion.org.uk

- write to SU Mail Order, PO Box 5148, Milton Keynes MLO, MK2 2YX